GW00372323

Hope in Darkness

HOPE IN DARKNESS

Poems of Sorrow and Comfort

Antioch Publishing Company
Yellow Springs, Ohio 45387
0-89954-775-3

CONTENTS

HOPE IN DARKNESS
Kevin Quinney

Do not weep,
Do not cry,
For my body is broken
But my spirit is heavenly.

Do not sorrow,
Do not mourn,
My body is broken
But my soul is peaceful.

Do not protest,
Do not be desolate,
For my soul is now a star.

Do not gaze sadly,
For I am an angel now.
Peace is mine
And in Heaven do I roam.

ON THE DEATH OF MY MOTHER

Sheelagh FitzGerald

Where are you now? You dear ones
Whose laughter I miss.
In what green fields do you wander
And what do your eyes behold?
Are you children again? Children of God
Listening to His wisdom?
Do you think of us, as we toil?
And will you welcome us when our time comes
To free the spirit from a tired body?
Sometimes, in some familiar place, we
Almost feel you near, making us sure
That death divides only by dimension.
Our eyes cannot see you, yet our hearts still
Know your presence.
This eternal mystery continues – it tests our
Faith.
For if there is no reunion – no joyful
Meeting again with those we have loved
So dearly,
Then, O God – why did You make us?
For what purpose – and in Your image?

THE MOST LOVING ACT OF ALL
Kenneth E. Carman

These precious moments, gems of life
That lift the heart and banish strife
Within the mind,
Calm the waters and kill the pain,
Reviving hope for love again.
Cool, calm evening, summer dawn,
Blown across the southern sky
Help to show the reason why
Her eyes stayed open
To feel the pines and smell the ferns,
Purple-blue heather.
Poor old body, frail, worn, yearns
To know whether
I am tasting the fresh misty morning air
Revealing early shadows, long,
Pale pink across the field.
Her gasping, raking breath did not yield.
Her pale blue gaze
Transcribing her final haze,
Lifting to reveal life and love,
Fulfilment far above –
    the ups and downs of her life.

She's gone, body and soul.
She gave me all her living, bequeathed me all
Her values,
To Heaven in my mind.
Trees, river banks, small crabs in sand,
Moth, spider, flowers, feathers in hand,
Her house upon a rock
    where she could no longer stand
Left to me. She did not fall
With me beside her final call
Forgave me all.
My dearest dear,
Not for me to stay the hand
That lifts the moon and sifts the sand.

PARTING
Glenda Mitchel Palmer

Christian friends – so sad to part;
A seed of love in each full heart,
Ready to bloom when Heaven they see;
Together, forever, in eternity.

AUTUMN IS HERE
Angela Upton Cheney

Autumn is here, old friend: today
I felt its presence on the summer air,
Sad that we can no more this moment share
Since on tired wings you homed away

To lovelier landscapes, there to find
The sum of all Octobers such as I
Can barely glimpse, beyond each fresh July
That you have left so far behind.

Together with those yearned-for, old
Great days when you would smile to hear me say,
'The tide has turned – autumn is on its way,
Laden with crimson and with gold.'

But just in case you might still catch
My voice across the void, I'll signal you
Autumn's return, just as I used to do,
And will maintain my annual watch

For Nature's secret heralding
To the lush-flowering earth, and my sixth sense,
That contrary to present evidence
Summer's already on the wing.

Though round me now the rose-scents blend
With incense of hot sun on new-mown grass,
As here I lie and watch the white clouds pass,
Autumn is here, is here, old friend. . . .

SYMPATHY
Kevin Dean

Though your grief be too deep for words
And too personal to share,
Do not keep it so
But when you are able
Let the sympathy of loving friends
Support you, even if only a little.

THE FINAL BLOW
Kevin Dean

I see him now, a quiet boy
Who loved to run and play;
I see him racing in the wind,
I see him every day.

I see him smile, receive his prize,
Then turn to wave to me.
I weep and ask myself again
Why should such things be?

At fourteen years to suddenly
Fall ill and quickly die,
He wasted as I held his hand.
Why should it be? Oh why?

My husband first and then my son;
I felt it was the end,
I never could recover to live
On, would never mend.

But slowly I have learned to hope
And now I wait to see
Once more the faces that I love,
Once more smiling at me.

The quiet boy who ran and played,
Who raced into the wind,
Who took his prize, then waved his hand
And turned to me and grinned.

WINDCHIMES
Glenda Mitchel Palmer

God shattered my plate-glass life,
Then he took the broken pieces
And made them into windchimes.

THE AWAKENING
Irene Hodgkinson

She sat by his bed, her eyes on his face,
Then her mind wandered, she gazed into space.
She saw a young man, in the prime of his life,
She remembered the day she became his wife.

She saw the pride when he held his first son.
She saw the love for his children, each one.
She saw his tired face at the end of each day,
He worked so hard, but that was his way.

They shared their joys, they shared their tears,
They shared their hopes, they shared their fears.
Her gaze came back to the man in the bed,
She wished she had tears, but they'd all been shed.

Then a nurse came and took her hand,
It was then she began to understand.
She turned again and looked at the bed,
But the man she'd cared for so long was dead.

The days went by so dull and drear,
If only the spring and sunshine were here.
Then the sun broke through the gloom,
Spring and summer would be here soon.

Suddenly she came to see,
All the things that were meant to be.
A time to live, a time to die,
Don't look at the ground, look up to the sky.

I see you in the gentle spring,
I hear you in the birds that sing.
I feel your caress as a breeze goes by,
I see you smile in a summer sky.

So I'll grieve no more for you, my dear,
Because I feel you're always near.
In the scent of the flowers, the beautiful trees,
The flight of the birds, the hum of the bees.

And thank you, my love, for giving to me
Your love of beauty, of all things free.
I've had my loss, I've had my pain.
But because of my faith, we'll meet again.

Of course, you've guessed that she was me.
Thank you, Lord, for helping me.

A Widow To Her Grandchild, Born The Week Of Her Bereavement

Dora M. Jay

Sweet new life,
You are to me a light that glows
In my darkest hour;
Though fate has closed a door
Behind me, your smile has opened
Windows on a new world,
Yet to be explored.
I look into your eyes and see
Before me hope and love to come;
I wait, to watch you grow
From babyhood to childhood,
And to hold your hand in mine
So we together can explore
Your world of wonderment and joy.
I can now fill my lonely hours
With thoughts of you, and dreams
Of happy years ahead,
And pray that as you grow
You will regard me as a friend.

TIME HEALS?
Kevin Dean

I looked into the old man's face,
Bewildered, wet with tears,
And saw pain and astonishment.
And after all these years
I see them still and I recall
The stupid words I said:
'Time heals, be patient and be strong,'
To one whose son was dead;
At twenty-five, a suicide,
None could imagine why,
With life so full of promise,
He should have sought to die.

The other night I had a dream:
The old man smiled at me,
'You're wrong, it's not in time we're healed,
But in eternity.'

SHE LEAVES A HUSBAND ...
Michael James

From some far-distant yesterday,
Comes now the scent of fresh-mown hay;
Sound of the lark's ascending trill,
And the wild strawberry's sweet taste still.
Golden to eye, the wave-lapped strand,
Gentle embrace of hand in hand.
Senses we shared, you and me;
Placed now in grateful memory.

I watched you die, yet no more cry,
But softly sigh in fond mind's eye;
See clear the place where first we met,
And where your daisied grave is set.
Long miles between them, years as well,
Two kinds of space, my senses tell.
Me here below, and you above;
Apart in place, bound firm in love.

To do God's will, I dwell here still,
His earth to till, my life fulfil.
Biology, geography,
Encompass not, it seems to me,
The fullest depths with which to know
What's meant by sense or place, and so,
In our true home for me, sweet, wait
For God to call me to His gate.

GOD'S SOFT LAWN
J. Dalmain

Gnarled and grey, frost-touched and forlorn,
Alone, the winter garden awaits
Rosebuds sweet that will soon adorn
Doorways and tangled rustic gates.
Even thus – in our darkest dawn –
Night lightens and shadow abates,
Sunshine smiles upon God's soft lawn . . .

Where joyful tranquillity waits.

DIARY OF A DEATH
Kevin Dean

Last night the clouds, red in the sunset,
Cleared the mountain-tops like leaping tigers
And a great white cloud of nameless shape
   was utterly still.

This morning the sky is white as the sunrise
And the silhouette of the mountains
Climbs and falls to that high peak
Where my mother lies close to Heaven, dying.

Across the water a wood in the form of a cross
Looks up and pleads,
A bell gently tolls,
Calls the gulls, the cuckoos, the doves
And a thousand other creatures
To cry aloud with me and beg that she
May enter eternal joy, beauty,
   delight and tranquillity.

Into Your hands, O Lord, I commit her
Through whom You breathed life into me.

PLEASE WAIT FOR ME
Irene Hodgkinson

Darling, it's now just a year
Since you left me for a while.
I've tried to carry on,
I've tried so hard to smile,
But when I miss you so, my dear,
My mind clouds over,
My thoughts aren't clear,
My memories are of all your pain.
But I couldn't wish you
Back here again.
So, my darling, just wait for me
To join you in eternity.

AN OLD LADY'S TEARS
Kevin Dean

Crossing the place we call The Bar
   she shook with tears in the back of the car.
Her thoughts were filled with her own dear boy,
   who was and is still her pride and joy.

'It's almost forty years ago
   and on this very day
That he died after Sunday school
   in such a tragic way.'

She sees him with his hair still wet
   from swimming in the stream,
A lad of eighteen years of whom
   she often still must dream.

For always in her talk he comes,
   cycling – he never walked;
She sees him stretched out on the road,
   bleeding as he talked.

'A gentle boy who would not kill
    a rabbit in a field –
Why should he die? she asks sometimes
    and to despair would yield.

'But look around at all these trees.
    How could they just appear?
My boy is in the hands of God,
    and he's worth every tear.'

'Just now and then I feel a doubt
    which places me in Hell,
Until I see the world God's made
    and know that all is well.'

THE LONG FIRST DAYS
J. Dalmain

Sad, empty, lonely, the long first days of grief,
Only tear-filled memories bring a kind relief –
Remembrance means we have love within us still.
Rest then – and remember that we always will.
One small step at a time through the darkest days;
Wait! And God will bring a lightening of your ways.

To My Son, Killed In An Accident
Sheelagh FitzGerald

The light that was your life
Has been extinguished.
The warmth of your sun no longer warms me,
The joy of your presence is not with me.

How shall I live without you?
Of course, I must.
At first it is like a sudden cripple –
Groping, blinded,
I see no beauty around me,
I feel and taste nothing – my laughter is
False, for there is no joy.

And yet it is not meant that my life
Should only be bathed in your reflection.
Gradually but surely, I must go forward,
Step by step building the days to a
Fulfilment that you knew.
Your colourful, busy, exciting life must
Be my inspiration.
You did not lean on me for your joys,
And neither must I.

God help me to fill my days with meaning
And again – in time – laughter,
So that when we meet again
You will be proud of me!

TRAVELLERS
Ruth Slater

We travel a different road,
My son and I.
For him, I must proceed with joy
Along a pathway of a different kind.
Striving to know that he is safe,
In a greater love than mine.
And surely, Lord, in this way
Will I my freedom find.

THE FUNERAL
Patricia M. Newton

The church seemed filled. There could have
    been more people.
Four priests stood there. He could have had
    fourteen.
The day was dry. The wind was harsh and
    stringent.
The sky grim grey, the grass reluctant green.
A wrong hymn sung – forgot to change the
    numbers,
Get someone to announce them if you can!
And yet – would all those details really matter
To this one simple faithful honest man?

The food so basic – pies, ham rolls and teacakes,
The clubroom drab and weary in its tone,
The voices forced, the eyes stiff shocked and
    sunken
That he could go and leave them on their own.
They somehow felt that he would last forever,
Eternal father of a mortal clan,
And here they were, forlorn in joy and triumph
Remembering one true and honest man.

He was an upright father, sternly righteous,
A man of God, of deep and simple prayer,
A human soul, aware of every weakness,
A penitent who lived to love and care.
A gentle Grandad, gazing at the youngsters
Who wondered if he ever walked or ran,
He had three legs – one fine, one stiff, one
    wooden,
This humorous and gentle honest man!

His children clung together – one was missing,
Aunts, cousins, nephews meeting after years,
The women sat, the men moved round in
    circles,
And soon some laughter came
    to frame the tears . . .
Remember when . . .? What happened . . .?
    Did he really . . .?
Did you believe it when it all began . . .?
And there among them, peaceful, half forgotten,
The quiet smile of one true honest man.

PAEAN
David Parrott

Goodbye, George.
Thanks a lot
For your witty humour,
Your little hop
As you pranced down the road.

Your chat on the Second Coming,
Knowing I was unbelieving,
Your Gilbertian tags and Latin quotations,
Your facility in Greek translations,
The eyeshade when the sun was bright,
Growing cataracts with failing sight
That never dimmed your eternal faith.
As the mystique of death about you glows
As now your soul into the universe flows,
Do we not all something from it gain,
For you were a truly christian Christian.

In Memoriam
Harold T. Pritchard

Farewell, dear friend, now passed
   beyond our sight,
To climb the stairway up to Heaven's gate;
It matters not if it be soon or late,
We too are destined to behold the light;
Together we shall share the home prepared,
Take up again the fellowship we shared
In our so brief encounter here below;
No vague hope this, faith tells us it is so.
Meanwhile, we cherish all we knew of you,
Courage in trouble, fortitude in pain,
The smile that broke through all adversity,
The evidence you did not live in vain.

O generous friend, though you be unaware,
We offer for your soul our chastened prayer.

PAIN
Karen Butler

A tear drops from the child's eye,
Years of pain caught up inside,
She cries so deeply from within
Hoping someone might hear her,
As things look bleak,
As if no one cares.
Through the tears she sees
You and Your loving face,
And then as she wipes her eyes
The tears just seem to fall,
As if inside the pain has changed
To an everlasting joy.
This is how it feels
When we give our lives to You.
The pain is just peeled off
And replaced with everlasting love.

PRAYER IN FAILURE
Kevin Dean

Thank you, Lord, although I've failed,
Passed over once again.
I feel upset and weary as I
Wonder if and when
I'll ever taste the joy of sweet
Success, feel blessed not cursed;
Just once to know I tried my best
And actually came first.

It doesn't really matter, Lord,
Just give me what you see
Is best all round to help me do
The task You've given to me.
They shall be first who once were last,
Who loved yet failed again,
For God requires a perfect heart,
Not mighty deeds, from men.

CONSOLATION
Laurence Ager

What's done is done, and nothing can restore
The happiness which I had known before.
Yet, should I grieve as one of hope bereft
When, despite all, sweet memory is left?

Suppose the happiness whose loss I mourn
Had never come my way, should I not find
A yawning blank filling the empty space
Where now is sweet remembrance in my mind?

Can I not tell myself that I was blessed
In sharing happiness till now untold?
And though some lovely part of it is gone,
Let me recall with thanks, and be consoled.

WAR MEMORIAL
Frances Dover

The life they lived here hasn't changed
Since those young ones marched away;
The village, slightly rearranged,
Still neatly wears their yesterday.

Spring the voice at the school playground,
The cricket field a summer song;
Autumn's crackle of social round,
Winter edging the new year along.

The breeze they felt still stirs the leaves,
The same rain falls through which they ran;
Martins seek the same old eaves,
The boy today, so soon the man.

And on the stone where the loss is told
The sun lights up their names in gold.

WILL THE PAIN GO?
Sheelagh FitzGerald

Will the pain go, when the well of tears
Runs dry?
Or will I carry the sound like some
Battle scar for ever in my heart?
God's gift to me taken away so soon,
Leaving only precious memories to
Help me through the long days and nights.
God, who sent the pain, O send me healing,
For I cannot bear the grief.

BEAUTY THAT HEALS
Kevin Dean

If you dwell on the hurt that is within
You will make of your heart a place
Of bitterness which will show in your eyes
And in time disfigure your face.

But open your eyes to the green hills
And the rays of the setting sun,
Open your ears to the sound of the sheep
And the lambs which jump and run,
And find a vastness within yourself,
    an insatiable appetite
For beauty which heals and reveals
Yourself,
Granting the gift of sight.

COMPASSION
Irene Hodgkinson

I feel so sorry for those
Who lose a loved one
And who believe
Their life is done.
They've just gone on
To a higher plane,
And if you've faith
You'll meet again.
So do not turn your head away
From believers when they say
They really are here with you,
Loving you still, as they used to do.
If you could accept this
You would be
Happy for them in eternity.
You see, by now they know
There's a higher life
Than here below.
I do hope you'll think again,
It will help you, ease your pain,
Until one day your call will come
To meet your loved one in God's Home.

GRIEF
Sheelagh FitzGerald

It lies within me, like a sword,
And wraps around my being like the
Cold sea mist.
Like the mist, it clears a little now and then,
But returns again as the incoming tide.
I almost welcome the rush of tears to bathe
My wounds in moisture,
To ease the dry ache that lives within me.
And yet the flow of tears that fall like rain,
A never-ending river, do not heal but leave
Me weary, drained and sad.
Only time, ticking relentlessly on, will give the
    cure.
For, as the days continue, so my own life
    approaches its end,
Which is also my beginning and our reunion.

PEACE
Ruth Slater

It's made of moments
Here and there.
Smiles and glances
I know not where.
Country walks,
Streams idling by,
A quiet lunch.
Let time pass by.
I know not why I enjoyed today:
Time is a healer,
This moment – I'm free!

THERE WAS A DAY
Sister Maree CHN

There was a day
When shadows moved across my face
And a candle ceased to burn.
When my gaze but saw a darkness,
And my world was wet with tears.
So fragile is a soul,
As gentle as a wild flower
That man so often treads,
As fragile as the setting sun that
Paints the Heavens pink,
But in a single moment fades from sight.
A shadow moved across my face
And a candle ceased to burn.
My love has gone
And my world was wet with tears.
But in the setting sun
I see a butterfly with wings
Of glorious pink.
Wild flowers grow across my path,
And a candle burns within my heart.

Tears
Maud Poulton

Tears are the heart's blood.
Remember this; and when they flow
Because life deals some bitter blow,
Know that this is good.

'Tis nature's way of healing pain,
But more than this; the tears that start
Are drops of blood from out the heart
Which are not shed in vain.

They are carried to Heaven from Earth,
Our tears are borne by angel bands,
And they are changed whilst in their hands
To pearls of priceless worth.

There in Heaven our treasure is.
The gems are laid to our account,
And according as our sorrows mount,
So, too, our future bliss.

Tears of blood mean sacrifice.
They are shed at such great cost,
But we must not think them lost,
They are worth the price.

A TIME FOR TRUTH
Gaynor D. Williams

In the silence there is comfort
From yesterday's despair.
In the stillness there is wisdom –
That only God can share.
In the darkness there is solitude,
All strife and turmoil cease,
In the gentle arms of night
There is sanctuary . . . and peace.

WINTER SORROW
BRINGS SPRING JOY
Katherine Osborne

Winter comes wildly in, relentlessly,
Withering the flowers that once played their part
To comfort and console the anxious heart,
Leaving bare branches on each shivering tree.

The biting wind and freezing snow contrive
To search out and attack unarmoured chinks,
And sever sadly our last longing links
With warmth of sun and fields with flowers alive.

Yet in the winter strength and joy abound:
The glory of a frosty moonlit night,
The unexpected shaft of sun-born light,
The star-shaped snowflakes scattering to the ground.

And winter finally must end its lease,
That spring may follow in its dying wake,
The spring of hope and love will come and make
The earth a vibrant place of joy and peace.

So must our lives sorrow like winter know,
The days of darkness and of solitude,
The hours when there seems nothing that is good,
The witless words that strike so sharp a blow.

But like the winter sorrow will depart,
God's peace and love will ease the troubled brain.
Who knows? We may find happiness again,
Helping to heal with love a bruisèd heart.

IN LOVING MEMORY
Frances Fry

Love is our reason for living,
When all is said.
Love keeps our memory living
After we're dead.

GATHER MY GRIEF
Myra Reeves

Gather my grief at the foot of Thine altar, Lord,
Where the sorrows of the earth are stored.
Hidden flame in the mist beyond the Cross,
Between Thy holy candles
   burn out all my dross.
Gather my grief to Thee,
Gather my grief.

Suffer Thy word to light upon me, Lord,
In the mystery of grace restored.
Hidden voice in the muted music heard.
Suffer me not to lose Thy life-illumining word.
And gather my grief to Thee,
Gather my grief.

Quicken my impulse with Thy wisdom, Lord,
That only harmony be love's reward.
Hidden beat in the pulse of all mankind,
Inspire the broken rhythm
   of my heart and mind.
And gather my grief to Thee,
Gather my grief.

GRIEVE, MY FRIEND
Ruth Slater

Take it out and look at it, your grief, my friend,
Allow the mask that keeps your countenance
    serene
To slip once in a while.

As with a precious gem, you polish and appraise
    its hue;
So will you glean, each time,
A different point of view.

Your grief is like the gem that sparkles with the
    light,
Its worth is untold, and serves to make you
    realise
That life is to be solved.

ALONE

Glenda Mitchel Palmer

I'm alone, but I'm not lonely,
For my Saviour is by my side.
The solid rock is my great comfort,
The morning star my only guide.

Walking up the paths to glory,
Jesus knows my every need;
God the Father holds the future,
The Holy Spirit takes the lead.

If you know deep pain and sorrow,
Joy is offered if you only
Take His hand and you will echo
I'm alone, but I'm not lonely.

Jamie, Blind And Deaf
J. Train

I can't see or hear you, but I can feel your touch,
And I can smell you, and I love you very much.
Why I was born thus no one seems to know.
For my loving parents what a bitter blow.
But I promise I'll never shoot a gun,
Never be a felon going on the run,
Never see a single vile or evil deed,
To spite and bitter words pay no heed.
All my life I will be sin-free,
Not many boys will be like me.
I can feel your heartbeat as you clutch me tight,
I can feel you crying in the middle of the night,
Your love and my love mingling as one.
I'm so glad that I'm your son.
Other boys are different – well, that's as may be.
I have other gifts, for I am Jamie.

LORD, LET ME THINK ON
LOVELY THINGS
Pearl Reynolds

Lord, let me think on lovely things,
Like days beside the sea,
And Jesus teaching on the shores
Of tranquil Galilee.

How at His touch the lame can walk,
The blind are made to see,
The deaf can hear, the sick are healed,
As He speaks lovingly.

And guilty souls are given rest,
Their sins are all forgiven.
He brings the outcast in to join
The family of Heaven.

I cannot leave this place to go
To lovely Galilee.
But in my sick-room I will wait
And He will come to me.

And at His touch I will be healed,
My eyes His glory see,
And He will make my heart be glad,
Now and eternally.

CRADLE SONG
Ettilie Wallace

I dreamed my father died last night
I did not dream a death-bed scene
Saw no casket
Saw no flowers
But in the chapel hall there stood
A simple cradle of brown wood
Long, strong and comfortable
Padded soft as for a babe newborn

In this he lay.

LIFE INTO DEATH INTO LIFE
Myra Reeves

It was a broken bird,
Hurt wings folded, forgotten how to fly,
Lost the blue air, the beyond,
Grounded;
Twittering against the healing hold
  of kind hands,
The voice saying, Be still,
Be at peace,
So it became at last.

Now they have opened wide
With what sweet grace!
The bird flew straight to the eye of Heaven,
It is flying, flying, flying
Into unnameable joy.
Blue freedom; the awakening sun,
Purged of its little pain
By a huge splendid universal surge of love
And grief immeasurable and deep humanity.

It flies on and on,
Singing with laughter and sweet delight
And life, life, life

O bird, fly on, fly on. . . .

NOVEMBER
Nita McCallum

Why should I weep, I who am left alone?
When I have God, Who is my all!

Why should I care, if life must pass me by?
But care I must, for each and all.

Quiet in my room with evening yet to come,
The noisy world is still without.

Softly my door shall open wide for all
To enter in and find His peace.

SORROW
Penn Everitt

When we walk the path
Of sorrow,
When we cannot face
Tomorrow,
For our loved one
Has departed into death:
Let us look unto the One
Who gave His only son
To die upon the cross
Broken-hearted.

Let Him take your hand and lead you
Into pastures green and new,
Where peace flowers in profusion
And love is gentle as the dew
That leaves its tender message
On everything you do –

'Lo, I am with you always, and
I will never leave you.'

See God's loving kindness
Turning loss into a gain,
Transforming every sorrow,
Transforming every pain.
Know God's loving kindness
Is forever there;
Bringing light out of the darkness
And faith out of despair!

HAIKU
John Martin

We weep for the dead;
Our tears watering the hope
To meet in Heaven.

GRIEF
Christine Michael

Your grief is not a thing in isolation
Therefore do not hold it in
Tight, caged up like a bird
That cannot sing.
Search carefully among your friends
And even those you do not know,
Find one you can trust,
Then let those tears flow . . .
Flow with the rhythms of feeling,
The surest tides of all,
Flow with the universe of healing,
The Lord God hears your call.

HAIKU
John Martin

Sorrow as well as joy
Comes from God. Accept them both
With equal embrace.

TEARS
Alice Fairclough

I have not shed all my tears.
True, some part I have spilled,
A libation, I hope,
To the unfathomable mystery of God.
And the rest I hold carefully
In the chalice of my inner being.
Let me keep that chalice safe for my Lord.
And oh, my Lord, I pray,
Put forth thy power once more;
Turn this water
Into the rich wine of compassion,
That I may bring it to Thy altar
For consecration.

AND AT THE END
Kevin Dean

And at the end
Let's not pretend
That time can mend wounds such as these;

But rather, at the last,
Look at the past,
Its shadows cast, with that of death to come

And realise
With what surprise
We shall arise to meet dear friends

And smile
To see serenity in every eye,
To understand how each life linked together,
To know that love brings peace,
To feel the beginning of joy.